THE STORY OF
CIVILIZATION

VOLUME I
THE ANCIENT WORLD

TEST BOOK

Copyright © 2016 TAN Books, PO Box 410487, Charlotte, NC 28241.

ISBN: 978-1-50510-569-8

Cataloging-in-Publication data on file with the Library of Congress.

Printed and bound in the United States of America.

TAN Books
Charlotte, North Carolina
www.TANBooks.com
2016

THE STORY OF
CIVILIZATION

VOLUME I
THE ANCIENT WORLD

From the Dawn of History
to the Conversion of Constantine

TEST BOOK
WITH ANSWER KEY

CONTENTS

A WORD TO THE TEACHER

This test book serves as a companion resource to *The Story of Civilization: The Ancient World*, authored by Phillip Campbell and brought to you by TAN Books. With this book, students can test their reading comprehension and further educate themselves on the content found in the text.

This volume covers the history of the world from the earliest nomads to the conversion of Emperor Constantine. Your students will learn what life was like in the ancient civilizations of Egypt, Mesopotamia, Persia, Greece, Rome, and more, as well as learn the Old Testament stories of the Israelites and the coming of Christ. They'll take a journey through the first days of the Church and see the courage the early Christians showed as they faced persecution and oppression.

The strength of *The Story of Civilization* lies not only in the exciting narrative style in which it retells the historical content but also in the way it presents history through the faithful prism of the Church. Have you always wanted your children to learn about world history from a Catholic perspective? Here, with the textbook and this companion test book, you'll have the trusted resources you've always wanted.

Enhanced Storytelling

The Story of Civilization reflects a new emphasis in presenting the history of the world as a thrilling and compelling story. Young people love a good story, and history is full of them: from the construction of the great pyramids in Egypt, to the training of young Spartan warriors, to the conquests of Alexander the Great, and the rise of mighty Rome.

The storytelling aspect of this series has been especially enhanced in several ways. First, the dynamic style of the new illustrations contributes powerfully to the narrative. Second, an audio recording of the text is available so students can enjoy the stories not just as readers but as listeners as well. This audio recording can assist young students who have not yet acquired the necessary reading vocabulary, as well as students who have reading disabilities. Lastly, the text itself contains short stories within each chapter that help explain the historical content to children. These stories work in conjunction with the facts, names, dates, and events presented in the text to convey the information in a fun and exciting way.

Using the Test Book

This book provides questions for each chapter that are suitable as a study exercise or as an objective answer test, with an answer key for teachers in the back. The questions include matching items, multiple choice, and true/false. Though not every test will contain all these types of questions, each test is based on a 100-point scale. Students should turn to each test after completing the corresponding textbook chapter and have parents grade it before moving on to the next. Roughly thirty minutes should be given to the student to complete each test, though that may vary depending on the child.

Be sure to visit www.TANBooks.com for more information and other companion products such as activity books, audio dramas, and video lectures.

CHAPTER 1
The Dawn of Civilization

Perfect Score: 100   Your Score: _____

True or False?

Directions: In the blank beside each statement, write "T" if the statement is *True* or "F" if the statement is *False*. Each correct answer is worth 5 points. 50 possible points.

_____ 1. Nomads lived in one place.

_____ 2. The world was a beautiful but frightening place for the early nomads.

_____ 3. The early nomads did not have writing.

_____ 4. Early people buried their dead with tools and other useful objects.

_____ 5. The early nomads lived a long life.

_____ 6. Farming, building cities, and writing are all signs of civilization.

_____ 7. The flooding of rivers was not good for the ancient people who farmed near them.

_____ 8. After people came together in cities, not everybody needed to farm.

_____ 9. Besides offering a source of life and water, rivers were also used for travel.

_____ 10. Writing was developed by farmers counting their animals.

Multiple Choice

Directions: For each numbered item, circle the letter beside the choice (A, B, C, or D) that best answers the question or completes the statement. Circle only one choice per item. Each correct answer is worth 5 points. 50 possible points.

1. How did nomads feed themselves?

A. by farming
B. by purchasing what they needed at the village market
C. by gathering seeds, nuts, and fruits and hunting wild animals
D. by robbing other villages

2. Scientists who dig up artifacts from the peoples of the past are called:

A. archaeologists.
B. paleontologists.
C. historians.
D. geologists.

3. How do we know the early nomads believed in an afterlife?

A. They wrote down their beliefs about the afterlife.
B. They carved pictures of heaven on cave walls.
C. They have come back from the dead to tell us about it.
D. They buried their dead with tools and things that would be useful.

4. Civilization really began when people started:

A. hunting for their food instead of gathering.
B. settling down to live in cities.
C. burying their dead in graves.
D. making tools.

5. A society that has become advanced and developed certain skills is called a:

A. tribe.
B. culture.
C. civilization.
D. people.

6. Where did the first civilizations develop?

A. in the mountains
B. near rivers
C. in the forests
D. on the plains

7. Shukallituda's garden kept failing because:

A. he could not keep it watered.
B. animals ate his seeds.
C. rival tribes destroyed it.
D. sun and wind were drying it out and blowing his seeds away.

8. People who traded goods between different cities were called:

A. merchants.
B. rulers.
C. nomads.
D. farmers.

9. This allowed ideas to be passed on from generation to generation.

A. metalworking
B. shipping
C. domesticating animals
D. writing

10. Which of the following is NOT a sign of civilization?

A. writing
B. living in cities
C. making weapons
D. farming

CHAPTER 2
The Gift of the Nile

Perfect Score: 100   Your Score: _____

Matching

Directions: In each blank beside a phrase, write the letter of the term that is described by that phrase. Each item is worth 5 points. 60 possible points.

A. Narmer   D. Narmer Palette   G. pharaoh   J. Upper Egypt
B. Amun-Ra   E. silt   H. hieroglyphics   K. Shaduf
C. the Nile   F. delta   I. Lower Egypt   L. beer

_____ 1. southern Egypt, filled with sloping desert hills and hardy warriors; its capital was Thebes

_____ 2. the great river of Egypt that made life possible for the ancient Egyptians

_____ 3. the Egyptian god of the sun

_____ 4. the picture-writing of the Egyptian priests

_____ 5. another name for the king of ancient Egypt

_____ 6. northern Egypt, near the Nile Delta; its capital was Memphis

_____ 7. first pharaoh of united Egypt

_____ 8. an ancient stone with carvings depicting Narmer's victory

_____ 9. the part of the Nile where it breaks into many smaller rivers and flows into the sea

_____ 10. dirt that is rich in nutrients; the Nile carries lots of it

_____ 11. the most popular drink in ancient Egypt

_____ 12. a bucket-like device used for getting water out of the Nile

Multiple Choice

Directions: For each numbered item, circle the letter beside the choice (A, B, C, or D) that best answers the question or completes the statement. Circle only one choice per item. Each correct answer is worth 5 points. 40 possible points.

1. What does King Narmer do as a sign of his victory over the conquered king?

A. grabs him by the hair and touches his forehead with a war club
B. ties him to a tree
C. makes him march ahead of his army
D. takes the blue crown away from him

2. Egypt is located in the northeastern continent of:

A. Asia.
B. Europe.
C. Mesopotamia.
D. Africa.

3. What makes the lands around the Nile so good for farming?

A. the mild and comfortable temperature
B. the yearly flooding of the Nile, which spreads silt across the land
C. the high amount of rainfall in Egypt
D. the complex system of canals built by Narmer

4. Which of the following was not one of the gods of ancient Egypt?

A. Amun-Ra
B. Abydos
C. Sobek
D. Hathor

5. Egyptian hieroglyphics were developed by Egypt's:

A. merchants.
B. farmers.
C. priests.
D. pharaohs.

6. The ancient Egyptians referred to their country as:

A. the Delta.
B. Upper Egypt.
C. the Nile.
D. the Two Lands.

7. The vast majority of people in ancient Egypt were:

A. priests.
B. merchants.
C. nobles.
D. farmers.

8. A common act Egyptians did to honor their gods was to:

A. whisper their name before going to sleep.
B. pour beer onto the ground of their home as an offering.
C. dress up in a costume that looked like the gods.
D. sing songs of praise.

CHAPTER 3
Egypt in the Pyramid Age

Perfect Score: 100   Your Score: _____

True or False?

Directions: In the blank beside each statement, write "T" if the statement is *True* or "F" if the statement is *False*. Each correct answer is worth 5 points. 25 possible points.

_____ 1. The earliest Egyptian dynasties come from a period called the *Old Kingdom.*

_____ 2. Mastabas were large, circular buildings where the body of the pharaoh was buried underneath.

_____ 3. The biggest pyramid ever constructed was the *Great Pyramid* of Giza.

_____ 4. The most important Egyptian buildings were all religious and either temples or tombs for the pharaohs.

_____ 5. The pharaohs wrote the *Book of the Dead,* which detailed how the burial rituals were to be carried out for them after they had died.

Multiple Choice

Directions: For each numbered item, circle the letter beside the choice (A, B, C, or D) that best answers the question or completes the statement. Circle only one choice per item. Each correct answer is worth 5 points. 75 possible points.

1. In ancient Egypt, a dynasty refers to a:

A. rectangular building used as a tomb.
B. family or kinship group that ruled the kingdom.
C. region over whom the pharaoh appointed a governor.
D. dead body treated so it would not decay.

2. The very first pyramid was built for which pharaoh?

A. Chephren
B. Khufu
C. Djoser
D. Pepi II

3. The earliest Egyptian tombs—large, rectangular buildings—were called:

A. pyramids.
B. sphinxes.
C. mummies.
D. mastabas.

4. The architect of the first pyramid was:

A. Imhotep.
B. Khufu.
C. Sobek.
D. Djoser.

5. The period of the earliest Egyptian dynasties is called the:

A. New Kingdom.
B. Middle Kingdom.
C. First Intermediate Period.
D. Old Kingdom.

6. Egyptians did not have a lot of wood, so they built their great buildings out of:

A. stone.
B. marble.
C. mud.
D. clay.

7. Egyptians believed that after death, their kings would live forever if:

A. their bodies were preserved.
B. their bodies were buried secretly and forgotten about.
C. their bodies were burned.
D. they paid enough money.

8. This was invented by stacking several mastabas on top of one another.

A. the Sphinx
B. a pyramid
C. a mummy
D. a super mastaba

9. The Great Pyramid of Egypt was built for this pharaoh.

A. Djoser
B. Imhotep
C. Chephren
D. Khufu

10. Why was the Sphinx built?

A. as a tomb
B. a statue of a god
C. a portrait of a pharaoh
D. nobody knows for sure

11. The *Book of the Dead* explained:

A. how to build a pyramid.
B. rituals and procedures to prepare a dead body for mummification and burial.
C. how to construct a mastaba.
D. the manners one must observe when talking to a pharaoh.

12. A nomarch was responsible for:

A. ruling a province, collecting taxes, and enforcing a pharaoh's decrees.
B. mummifying deceased pharaohs.
C. keeping guard over the tombs of the kings.
D. serving the pharaoh in his household.

13. This pharaoh reigned for ninety-four years.

A. Djoser
B. Khufu
C. Narmer
D. Pepi II

14. A *nome* is another word for:

A. the pharaoh.
B. the governor of a province who governed it on behalf of the pharaoh.
C. a region or province of Egypt.
D. a mastaba.

15. Toward the end of the Old Kingdom, the unity of Egypt began to break apart because:

A. Egypt was invaded by foreigners from Asia.
B. the nomarchs became too powerful and the pharaohs too weak.
C. a series of famines, plagues, and droughts struck the land.
D. two Egyptian dynasties began warring against each other.

CHAPTER 4
The Land Between Two Rivers

Perfect Score: 100   Your Score: _____

True or False?

Directions: In the blank beside each statement, write "T" if the statement is *True* or "F" if the statement is *False*. Each correct answer is worth 5 points. 50 possible points.

_____ 1. A pharaoh celebrated 30 years on the throne with a Sed festival.

_____ 2. The climate in Mesopotamia is much hotter and dryer than Egypt.

_____ 3. The two great rivers of Mesopotamia are the Tigris and the Euphrates.

_____ 4. The first civilization in Mesopotamia was that of the Akkadians.

_____ 5. Cities were much more important in Mesopotamia than in Egypt.

_____ 6. Cuneiform writing was invented not by priests but by merchants.

_____ 7. The Sumerians were conquered and unified by the Akkadians.

_____ 8. The world's first major law code was written by Sargon.

_____ 9. Sargon unified all the Sumerian cities into a single kingdom.

_____ 10. Mesopotamia means "Gift of the Nile."

Multiple Choice

Directions: For each numbered item, circle the letter beside the choice (A, B, C, or D) that best answers the question or completes the statement. Circle only one choice per item. Each correct answer is worth 5 points. 50 possible points.

1. Mesopotamia is located in:

A. northeastern Africa.
B. east Asia.
C. west Asia.
D. northwestern Africa.

2. The first people to build sailboats, domesticate animals, and develop irrigation were the:

A. Amorites.
B. Kassites.
C. Akkadians.
D. Sumerians.

3. Originally, each Mesopotamian city was independent and ruled by its own king. These were called:

A. ziggurats.
B. city-states.
C. Seds.
D. nomes.

4. These structures were at the center of Mesopotamian cities and dedicated as temples to the city's gods.

A. mastabas
B. pyramids
C. ziggurats
D. lapis lazuli

5. The word "cuneiform" means:

A. wedge shaped.
B. priest writing.
C. symbol writing.
D. merchant counting.

6. An epic is a:

A. religious story about the origin of the world.
B. song meant to be sung in the halls of a king.
C. myth about how a city got its patron god.
D. poem or story about the deeds of a great hero.

7. The Mesopotamian hero Gilgamesh is seeking:

A. to conquer seven cities.
B. the secret of eternal life.
C. to slay a great serpent.
D. to take his place among the gods.

8. Around 2270 B.C., this group invaded Mesopotamia.

A. Kassites
B. Sumerians
C. Akkadians
D. Egyptians

9. This king was the first ruler to unite the cities of Mesopotamia.

A. Sargon
B. Gilgamesh
C. Hammurabi
D. Merniptah

10. Hammurabi, King of Babylon, is most well known for:

A. constructing the greatest ziggurat in Mesopotamia.
B. building tremendous walls around Babylon.
C. growing rich in the trade of lapis lazuli.
D. issuing an important law code.

CHAPTER 5
Egyptian Empires

Perfect Score: 100   Your Score: _____

Matching

Directions: In each blank beside a phrase, write the letter of the term that is described by that phrase. Each item is worth 5 points. 50 possible points.

A. Senusret   E. Hatshepsut   I. Rameses II
B. trade routes   F. Thutmose III   J. Battle of Kadesh
C. Hyksos   G. chariot
D. Canaan   H. tribute

_____ 1. the hilly country between Mesopotamia and Egypt

_____ 2. a small cart pulled by a team of horses; used by the Egyptians for war

_____ 3. the most powerful pharaoh of the Middle Kingdom

_____ 4. famous fight between Rameses II and the Hittites

_____ 5. a road or path used by merchants to get their goods from one place to another

_____ 6. Asian invaders who ruled Egypt for several centuries

_____ 7. queen of Egypt who called herself pharaoh and wore a fake beard

_____ 8. one of Egypt's greatest pharaohs; fought and later made a peace treaty with the Hittites

_____ 9. great warrior-king; the son of Hatshepsut

_____ 10. money that one people or kingdom gives to another as a sign of submission

Multiple Choice

Directions: For each numbered item, circle the letter beside the choice (A, B, C, or D) that best answers the question or completes the statement. Circle only one choice per item. Each correct answer is worth 5 points. 50 possible points.

1. During the Middle Kingdom:

A. the nomarchs took all the power from pharaoh.
B. the pharaoh took all the power from the nomarchs.
C. the pharaoh and the nomarchs shared power.
D. nomarchs and the pharaoh were both conquered by the Hittites.

2. Egyptian trade routes to Mesopotamia passed through:

A. Canaan.
B. Sumer.
C. Asia Minor.
D. the Delta.

3. What did the Hyksos have that gave them an advantage over the Egyptians in battle?

A. mules
B. chariots
C. bows
D. horses

4. After the Hyksos were driven out of Egypt, the Egyptians realized that they needed to:

A. be skilled and powerful warriors.
B. engage in their own wars of conquest.
C. use horses.
D. all of the above.

5. The period after the fall of the Hyksos is called the:

A. Middle Kingdom.
B. New Kingdom.
C. Old Kingdom.
D. Really Old Kingdom.

6. This New Kingdom pharaoh sent a trading expedition into Africa and built many splendid monuments.

A. Senusret
B. Thutmose III
C. Hatshepsut
D. Rameses II

7. The most famous building constructed by Hatshepsut, which still exists today, is her:

A. mortuary temple.
B. step pyramid.
C. capital city of Pi-Rameses.
D. granary.

8. This pharaoh went to war seventeen times and controlled the trade routes between Egypt and Mesopotamia.

A. Rameses II
B. Pepi II
C. Tutankhamun
D. Thutmose III

9. This pharaoh led Egypt in the massive Battle of Kadesh with the Hittites.

A. Hatshepsut
B. Rameses II
C. Thutmose III
D. Khufu

10. Shortly after the death of Rameses II, New Kingdom Egypt:

A. suffered from famine, drought, and invasion and finally collapsed.
B. conquered Mesopotamia.
C. grew to its greatest power.
D. was conquered by the Hyksos.

CHAPTER 6
Peoples of the Levant

Perfect Score: 100   Your Score: _____

True or False?

Directions: In the blank beside each statement, write "T" if the statement is *True* or "F" if the statement is *False*. Each correct answer is worth 5 points. 75 possible points.

_____ 1. The Levant is the strip of land at the far eastern end of the Mediterranean Sea.

_____ 2. The chief official of the pharaoh's household was called the vizier.

_____ 3. Hattusa was the capital of Canaan.

_____ 4. The Hittites left many monuments and writings behind that tell us a lot about them.

_____ 5. Until 1893, archaeologists were not certain the Hittites ever existed.

_____ 6. *Tells* are great Canaanite hills with cities on top of them.

_____ 7. Baal, Moloch, and Astarte were the three main gods of the Hittites.

_____ 8. The Phoenicians lived in the cities of Tyre and Sidon.

_____ 9. In an alphabet, each symbol stands for a sound instead of an idea.

_____ 10. The Canaanite city-states were all united into a single kingdom.

_____ 11. The Canaanites were seldom left alone. Their cities were often attacked.

_____ 12. The Hittites were known for their cedar trees.

_____ 13. The Phoenicians were Canaanites.

_____ 14. The Hittite empire was never very large or powerful.

_____ 15. It is easier to learn a pictographic language than an alphabetic language.

Multiple Choice

Directions: For each numbered item, circle the letter beside the choice (A, B, C, or D) that best answers the question or completes the statement. Circle only one choice per item. Each correct answer is worth 5 points. 25 possible points.

1. The area of land known as the Levant connects:

A. Canaan and Mesopotamia.
B. Asia Minor and Canaan.
C. Egypt and Canaan.
D. Egypt and Mesopotamia.

2. This chapter's story explains how the Hittites conducted a peace treaty with the Egyptians by giving their princess in marriage to this pharaoh.

A. Rameses II
B. Thutmose III
C. Rameses III
D. Khamun-Ra

3. An important Canaanite tribe that lived by the sea and became merchants were the:

A. Hittites.
B. Phoenicians.
C. Anatolians.
D. Gezerites.

4. This King of Tyre made an alliance with King Solomon of Israel and helped him build the Temple of Jerusalem.

A. Hattusilis
B. Bentresh
C. Hiram
D. Yuny

5. The most important contribution of the Phoenicians was their:

A. cuneiform.
B. alphabet.
C. pictographs.
D. cedar trees.

CHAPTER 7
The God of Israel

Perfect Score: 100   Your Score: _____

Multiple Choice

Directions: For each numbered item, circle the letter beside the choice (A, B, C, or D) that best answers the question or completes the statement. Circle only one choice per item. Each correct answer is worth 5 points. 100 possible points.

1. In the ancient world, the largest and most beautiful structures were all:

A. royal palaces.
B. religious.
C. fortresses.
D. trading centers.

2. One of the first people to hear from God was this father of the Hebrews.

A. Hammurabi
B. Moses
C. Joseph
D. Abraham

3. The story of Abraham and his descendants is told in the biblical book of:

A. Genesis.
B. Exodus.
C. Judges.
D. John.

4. Despite the wealth of Abraham, he was sad because:

A. his wife Sarah could not have children.
B. his only son had died.
C. his wife Sarah had died when she was still young.
D. his wife Sarah could not cook well.

5. God promised this land to Abraham and his descendants.

A. Phoenicia
B. Ur
C. Canaan
D. Chaldea

6. The son of Abraham and Sarah was:

A. Jacob.
B. Isaac.
C. Esau.
D. Joseph.

7. Abraham, Isaac, and Jacob are called Patriarchs because:

A. they each had many sons.
B. they were the fathers of the Canaanite people.
C. they were bishops of important cities.
D. they were the fathers of the Israelite people.

8. A famine means:

A. there was no rain for a long time.
B. there was a shortage of food.
C. there was disease spreading throughout the land.
D. there was a series of destructive wars.

9. In order to escape the famine, the children of Israel went down into:

A. Egypt.
B. Canaan.
C. Hattusa.
D. Sumer.

10. The pharaoh of Egypt ordered all the Hebrew male children to be:

A. circumcised.
B. enslaved.
C. thrown into the Nile.
D. given one gold piece each.

11. Moses' encounter with God in the burning bush is recorded in the biblical book of:

A. Genesis.
B. Exodus.
C. Leviticus.
D. Deuteronomy.

12. How did the Israelites escape Egypt?

A. They battled their way out.
B. They walked out over the desert by following the trade routes.
C. They sailed from the Delta to Canaan.
D. God parted the waters of the Red Sea and allowed them to cross.

13. These rules taught the Israelites that God wanted them to worship Him alone and explained the laws by which He expected them to govern themselves.

A. Code of Hammurabi
B. Code of Moses
C. Ten Commandments
D. Beatitudes

14. When God speaks directly to man with a message He intends all people to know, it is called:

A. Divine Revelation.
B. the Bible.
C. prophecy.
D. divine intervention.

15. The pharaoh at the time of Moses was:

A. Thutmose III.
B. Rameses II.
C. Amenhotep III.
D. nobody knows for certain.

16. When the three messengers from God visited Sarah, they told her that:

A. her children would be slaves in Egypt.
B. her husband would die soon.
C. she would give birth to twin daughters.
D. in about a year, she would give birth to a son.

17. God told Abraham to take his wife, his flocks, and all his wealth and:

A. leave Mesopotamia.
B. sacrifice them.
C. take them down into Egypt.
D. leave Canaan.

18. This is found everywhere in human culture.

A. writing
B. warfare
C. peace
D. religion

19. He was raised in the court of pharaoh, but he eventually had to flee from Egypt.

A. Abraham
B. Moses
C. Jacob
D. Jochebed

20. When Moses asks God what His name is, God says His name is:

A. Jesus.
B. the Holy Trinity.
C. "I AM WHO I AM."
D. El Shaddai.

CHAPTER 8
The Kingdom of David

Perfect Score: 100   Your Score: _____

True or False?

Directions: In the blank beside each statement, write "T" if the statement is *True* or "F" if the statement is *False*. Each correct answer is worth 4 points. 40 possible points.

_____ 1. The story of the wandering of the Israelites is told in Leviticus, Deuteronomy, and Numbers.

_____ 2. It was Moses who led the Israelites into the land of Canaan.

_____ 3. When archaeologists dug up Jericho, they found the walls had collapsed just as the Bible said.

_____ 4. David was the first King of Israel.

_____ 5. David took power after Saul and his sons were slain in battle.

_____ 6. David made Jerusalem the capital of Israel.

_____ 7. King Solomon built a temple for God in Jerusalem.

_____ 8. Rehoboam was a popular king beloved by the Israelite people.

_____ 9. The northern Kingdom of Israel was ruled by the descendants of David.

_____ 10. God tried to warn the Israelites of their evil by sending prophets.

Matching

Directions: In each blank beside a phrase, write the letter of the term that is described by that phrase. Each item is worth 4 points. 60 possible points.

A. conquest
B. Joshua
C. Messiah
D. prophet
E. Old Testament

F. Saul
G. Nebuchadnezzar
H. City of David
I. Jericho
J. Ark of the Covenant

K. Rehoboam
L. Book of Joshua
M. Jeremiah
N. Assyrians
O. captivity

_____ 1. This Babylonian king conquered the Kingdom of Judah in 587 B.C.

_____ 2. He led the Israelites into the Promised Land and helped them conquer Canaan.

_____ 3. a special kind of priest-king that God would send to His people

_____ 4. another name for Joshua's wars to take over Canaan

_____ 5. the first King of Israel; killed in battle by the Philistines

_____ 6. This city's walls collapsed after Joshua marched around it with the Ark.

_____ 7. another name for Jerusalem

_____ 8. a person inspired by God to speak on his behalf

_____ 9. the history of God's dealings with the Israelites

_____ 10. another name for when people are taken as prisoners

_____ 11. son of Solomon; taxed his people too heavily

_____ 12. a prophet who was thrown into a well by King Zedekiah

_____ 13. they wiped out the Kingdom of Israel in 722 B.C.

_____ 14. a special golden box that contained the tablets of the Ten Commandments

_____ 15. book describing the conquest of Canaan by the Israelites

CHAPTER 9
The Bearded Kings of the North

Perfect Score: 100   Your Score: _____

True or False?

Directions: In the blank beside each statement, write "T" if the statement is *True* or "F" if the statement is *False*. Each correct answer is worth 5 points. 50 possible points.

_____ 1. The Assyrians originally came into Mesopotamia with the Akkadians.

_____ 2. Assyrian warriors often fought from horseback.

_____ 3. Assyrians did not like to hunt.

_____ 4. The Assyrians thought if they were nice enough to their conquered foes, people would want to make alliances with them.

_____ 5. The greatest city and capital of Assyria was Assur.

_____ 6. Sennacherib attacked Jerusalem, but he had to return home when a plague broke out among his soldiers.

_____ 7. The peoples of the Levant liked living under the Assyrians.

_____ 8. Nabopolassar of Babylon led the revolt against Assyria.

_____ 9. Nineveh was so completely destroyed that people wondered if it had ever existed.

_____ 10. The Assyrians conquered Jerusalem but failed to conquer Egypt.

Multiple Choice

Directions: For each numbered item, circle the letter beside the choice (A, B, C, or D) that best answers the question or completes the statement. Circle only one choice per item. Each correct answer is worth 5 points. 50 possible points.

1. This Assyrian king famously hunted dolphins and hippos in the Mediterranean.

A. Arvad
B. Tiglath-Pileser
C. Sennacherib
D. Assurbanipal

2. The Assyrians were able to beat cities into submission because of their:

A. horses.
B. bows.
C. battering ram.
D. beards.

3. The capital of Assyria was:

A. Nineveh.
B. Assur.
C. Samaria.
D. Babylon.

4. This was the practice of forcing conquered peoples to leave their homeland.

A. circumcision
B. deportation
C. deposition
D. defenestration

5. Assyrian power reached its height under King:

A. Tiglath-Pileser.
B. Ashurnasirpal.
C. Assurbanipal.
D. Shalmaneser III.

6. To beautify Nineveh, King Assurbanipal built a great:

A. museum.
B. artificial river.
C. wall.
D. library.

7. A kind of sculpture where figures are carved so they are higher than the surrounding material is called:

A. pottery.
B. relief.
C. fresco.
D. mosaic.

8. Shalmaneser V conquered the Israelite city of:

A. Samaria.
B. Jerusalem.
C. Jericho.
D. Megiddo.

9. The Assyrians are named after:

A. Assurbanipal.
B. their god, Assur.
C. the city of Assur.
D. Ashurnasirpal.

10. The homeland of the Assyrians was north of the Tigris River in:

A. Anatolia.
B. Canaan.
C. Egypt.
D. Mesopotamia.

CHAPTER 10
The Splendor of Babylon

Perfect Score: 100   Your Score: _____

True or False?

Directions: In the blank beside each statement, write "T" if the statement is *True* or "F" if the statement is *False*. Each correct answer is worth 4 points. 20 possible points.

_____ 1. The Assyrians were not only obeyed but also loved.

_____ 2. Nebuchadnezzar built the Hanging Gardens to please his mother.

_____ 3. Nebuchadnezzar restored Babylon's ancient ziggurat.

_____ 4. Nebuchadnezzar captured and destroyed Jerusalem.

_____ 5. The Persians were able to capture Babylon easily by blocking up the river.

Matching

Directions: In each blank beside a phrase, write the letter of the term that is described by that phrase. Each item is worth 4 points. 40 possible points.

A. Nabopolassar   F. Hanging Gardens
B. Assyrians   G. Necho II
C. vassals   H. Zedekiah
D. Nebuchadnezzar   I. Jerusalem
E. Amytis   J. Persians

_____ 1. those who owe allegiance and pay tribute to another kingdom

_____ 2. governor of Babylon who led the alliance that overthrew Assyria

_____ 3. pharaoh defeated by Nebuchadnezzar at the Battle of Carchemish

_____ 4. overthrown by the Babylonians

question continued on next page ➡

_____ 5. conquered Babylon sometime after the death of Nebuchadnezzar

_____ 6. last Israelite king of Judah

_____ 7. median wife of King Nebuchadnezzar

_____ 8. son of Nabopolassar and king of Babylon

_____ 9. conquered and destroyed by Babylon in 587 B.C.

_____ 10. these were constructed for Amytis by Nebuchadnezzar

Multiple Choice

Directions: For each numbered item, circle the letter beside the choice (A, B, C, or D) that best answers the question or completes the statement. Circle only one choice per item. Each correct answer is worth 4 points. 40 possible points.

1. How did the peoples of the Levant feel about the Assyrians?

A. They were loved for their gentleness.
B. They were loved because of their just laws.
C. They were feared because they were cruel and harsh.
D. They were feared because their beards were scary.

2. The Assyrian Empire was defeated by an alliance led by:

A. Nebuchadnezzar.
B. Nabopolassar.
C. Assurbanipal.
D. Necho II.

3. When a kingdom owes allegiance and pays tribute to another kingdom, they are called:

A. serfs.
B. satraps.
C. vassals.
D. nomes.

4. In order to rule better, the Babylonians:

A. brought youths from around their empire to be educated in Babylon.
B. killed their captives and deported defeated populations.
C. used battering rams to destroy the walls of conquered cities.
D. learned the languages of all the kingdoms they conquered.

5. The son and successor of Nabopolassar was:

A. Nabopolassar II.
B. Tiglath-Pileser.
C. Nineveh.
D. Nebuchadnezzar.

6. King Zedekiah of Judah:

A. allied with the Assyrians against Nabopolassar.
B. revolted against Nebuchadnezzar, was defeated, and lost his throne.
C. revolted against Nebuchadnezzar and succeeded.
D. conquered Babylon by damming up the Euphrates River.

7. Nebuchadnezzar made a peace treaty with his neighbors the:

A. Medes.
B. Persians.
C. Hittites.
D. Assyrians.

8. According to legend, the Hanging Gardens of Babylon were constructed because:

A. Nebuchadnezzar wanted to build something more impressive than a ziggurat.
B. Nebuchadnezzar was a gardener in his spare time.
C. Nabopolassar wanted to impress the people of Babylon.
D. Amytis, wife of Nebuchadnezzar, desired to see mountains.

9. Which of the following was NOT one of Nebuchadnezzar's building projects?

A. rebuilding the ziggurat of Etemenanki
B. building up the walls of Babylon
C. constructing the great library of Nineveh
D. building the Hanging Gardens

10. Belshazzar, last King of Babylon, did this during the Persian siege.

A. played the fiddle
B. led the army into battle
C. prayed in the temple
D. had a big party

CHAPTER 11
The Rise of Persia

Perfect Score: 100   Your Score: _____

True or False?

Directions: In the blank beside each statement, write "T" if the statement is *True* or "F" if the statement is *False*. Each correct answer is worth 5 points. 50 possible points.

_____ 1. The whole story of the ancient world is essentially about kingdoms conquering kingdoms.

_____ 2. In Daniel's vision, kingdoms were represented by wild animals fighting each other.

_____ 3. Cyrus was a cruel and unjust king.

_____ 4. The Jews hated Cyrus because he kept them in captivity.

_____ 5. The Persian attack on the Egyptian oasis Siwa was successful for King Cambyses.

_____ 6. Satraps were governors for the small sections that Persia had been divided into.

_____ 7. The Immortals were the best Persian soldiers, chosen to protect the king in battle.

_____ 8. Persia's army consisted only of Persians.

_____ 9. The Persians were related to the Medes.

_____ 10. Persia was the largest and best-organized ancient empire thus far.

Multiple Choice

Directions: For each numbered item, circle the letter beside the choice (A, B, C, or D) that best answers the question or completes the statement. Circle only one choice per item. Each correct answer is worth 5 points. 50 possible points.

1. The prophet who saw the vision of the changing kingdoms was:

A. Isaiah.
B. Daniel.
C. Ezekiel.
D. Jeremiah.

2. King Cyrus brought together the kingdom of the Persians and the kingdom of the:

A. Medes.
B. Egyptians.
C. Israelites.
D. Spartans.

3. After Cyrus' reign, the only place not under Persia's control was:

A. Babylon.
B. Egypt.
C. Israel.
D. Assyria.

4. The satrap system was instituted by which king?

A. Xerxes
B. Cyrus
C. Cambyses
D. Darius

5. The Persian religion taught that:

A. the Holy Trinity existed.
B. Zeus was the supreme ruler of all.
C. earth was a battleground between a good god and a bad god.
D. the Valkyrie and Odin watched over every battle.

6. What happened to the Persian army sent to conquer Siwa in Egypt?

A. They disappeared.
B. They won the battle.
C. They lost the battle.
D. They got lost and had to return home.

7. The Old Testament calls Cyrus:

A. an anti-Christ.
B. a shepherd.
C. a vassal.
D. a warlord.

8. Cyrus was the:

A. grandson of the last Median King Astyages.
B. son of the last Median King Astyages.
C. brother to the Persian King Xerxes.
D. father of the Persian King Belshazzar.

9. The Royal Road was a:

A. prime spot for robbers to steal from royalty.
B. river that boats would use to travel everywhere.
C. road that enabled messengers to travel quickly through the empire.
D. special shortcut through mountains used only by the king.

10. King Cambyses was succeeded by:

A. Darius' son.
B. Cyrus' brother.
C. Darius' brother.
D. Cyrus' son.

CHAPTER 12
People of the Isles

Perfect Score: 100   Your Score: _____

Matching

Directions: In each blank beside a phrase, write the letter of the term that is described by that phrase. Each item is worth 5 points. 50 possible points.

A. Crete
B. Minoans
C. Mycenaeans
D. Knossos
E. bull jumping

F. the *Iliad*
G. Sir Arthur Evans
H. King Minos
I. Greece
J. frescoes

_____ 1. warrior people who dominated Greece and the surrounding islands

_____ 2. great epic work of Homer about the Trojan War

_____ 3. peaceful inhabitants of Crete who built Knossos

_____ 4. paintings done on the plaster of walls or ceilings

_____ 5. the long, fertile island that was home to the Minoans

_____ 6. mythical ruler of Crete who built the labyrinth to imprison the minotaur

_____ 7. beautiful Minoan place on Crete; most likely destroyed by an earthquake

_____ 8. the center of Mycenaean culture

_____ 9. British archeologist who discovered Knossos in 1900

_____ 10. dangerous but entertaining Minoan sport

True or False?

Directions: In the blank beside each statement, write "T" if the statement is *True* or "F" if the statement is *False*. Each correct answer is worth 5 points. 50 possible points.

_____ 1. Young Minoan children would often leap over bulls as a form of entertainment.

_____ 2. The Mycenaeans didn't like to pillage and preferred to stay in their own land.

_____ 3. The people of the Levant knew all about the people of the Isles.

_____ 4. Crete is a barren and desolate island.

_____ 5. Reliefs are paintings done on the plaster of walls and ceilings.

_____ 6. It is unknown where the Minoans came from originally.

_____ 7. Greece is a long, narrow island in the Mediterranean Sea.

_____ 8. Knossos was probably destroyed by pirates.

_____ 9. The frescoes in Crete depicted everyday life, not great battles.

_____ 10. The great city of the Mycenaeans was Mycenae.

CHAPTER 13
The Founding of Greece

Perfect Score: 100

Your Score: _____

Multiple Choice

Directions: For each numbered item, circle the letter beside the choice (A, B, C, or D) that best answers the question or completes the statement. Circle only one choice per item. Each correct answer is worth 5 points. 50 possible points.

1. Daedalus was:

A. the inventor who built the labyrinth.
B. a foolish boy who flew too close to the sun.
C. a king who imprisoned a boy and his father.
D. a monster in a maze that devoured all who entered.

2. In passing from Crete to Greece, we move into the continent of:

A. Asia Minor.
B. America.
C. Europe.
D. Africa.

3. Greece is:

A. an island.
B. a peninsula.
C. a mountain.
D. a city.

4. The Mycenaeans were:

A. farmers.
B. fisherman.
C. rich and fat.
D. great warriors.

5. The people who came to live in Greece around 1100 B.C. were called:

A. Spartans.
B. Athenians.
C. Dorians.
D. Indians.

6. Instead of writing things down, the early Greeks would:

A. draw pictures.
B. memorize their history in epic poems.
C. mime.
D. forget everything.

7. The poet Homer is said to have composed:

A. the *Iliad* and the *Odyssey*.
B. the *Aeneid* and the *Iliad*.
C. the *Odyssey* and the *Aeneid*.
D. the Bible and the Book of Kells.

8. The Trojan War began because:

A. Odysseus killed the Trojan king.
B. Helen, queen of Sparta, was kidnapped by the Trojans.
C. the Trojans destroyed a large wooden horse.
D. Homer refused to tell stories to the Trojan king.

9. A *labyrinth* is a:

A. kind of long sword.
B. device for breaking into cities.
C. short poem.
D. large maze.

10. Who won the Trojan War?

A. the Trojans
B. the Persians
C. the Greeks
D. the Israelites

True or False?

Directions: In the blank beside each statement, write "T" if the statement is *True* or "F" if the statement is *False*. Each correct answer is worth 5 points. 50 possible points.

_____ 1. Icarus and Daedalus fled from King Menelaus of Sparta.

_____ 2. Greece has bad farmland but good soil for growing olives and figs and grazing livestock.

_____ 3. The Dorians were tall with long, reddish hair.

_____ 4. The Mycenaeans and Dorians would intermarry and become the Greeks.

_____ 5. Odysseus came up with the plan to trick the Trojans into opening their gates.

_____ 6. The *Iliad* tells the story of the Trojan War.

_____ 7. Homer was the most famous of all Greek poets.

_____ 8. The *Odyssey* is the story of Odysseus' journey home after the Trojan War.

_____ 9. Homer's poems were never written down and only survive today by word of mouth.

_____10. "The Greek Dark Ages" was a period where the sun never shone on the crops in Crete.

CHAPTER 14
Greek Mythology

Perfect Score: 100   Your Score: _____

Matching

Directions: In each blank beside a phrase, write the letter of the term that is described by that phrase. Each item is worth 5 points. 50 possible points.

A. Hera   F. Hades
B. Poseidon   G. Apollo
C. Athena   H. Artemis
D. Aphrodite   I. Hermes
E. Zeus   J. Dionysius

_____ 1. goddess of wisdom and patron of Athens

_____ 2. king of all the gods

_____ 3. messenger of the gods

_____ 4. god of knowledge and light; very popular

_____ 5. god of wine

_____ 6. queen of the gods and Zeus' sister

_____ 7. Zeus' brother and god of the ocean

_____ 8. goddess of love

_____ 9. Zeus' brother and lord of the underworld

_____10. goddess of animals, hunters, virgins, and children; Apollo's twin sister

Multiple Choice

Directions: For each numbered item, circle the letter beside the choice (A, B, C, or D) that best answers the question or completes the statement. Circle only one choice per item. Each correct answer is worth 5 points. 50 possible points.

1. Hephaestus was the god of:

A. war.
B. fish.
C. agriculture and cows.
D. fire and craftsmanship.

2. Demeter was the goddess of:

A. marriage.
B. grain and harvest.
C. swans.
D. rivers and streams.

3. Ares was the god of:

A. war.
B. wolves.
C. kings.
D. stars.

4. Olympus is:

A. the mountain on which the gods live.
B. the river that runs below the palace of the gods.
C. Hera's favorite peacock.
D. Zeus' prize thunderbolt.

5. A myth is:

A. a short poem of Homer's invention.
B. a craggy mountain pass used by Hermes to carry messages quickly.
C. an invented story to explain a certain truth in the world.
D. a song sung by Artemis every night to put her nymphs to sleep.

6. In the story of Theseus and the Minotaur, what happened every nine years in Athens?

A. The Minotaur was used for bull jumping instead of an ordinary bull.
B. Seven boys and seven girls were sent to Crete to be killed in the labyrinth.
C. Theseus killed a replica of the Minotaur.
D. The labyrinth was opened for anyone wishing to challenge Theseus, the monster that lived inside.

7. Who fell in love with Theseus?

A. Andromeda
B. Aphrodite
C. Ariadne
D. Arachne

8. How did Theseus find his way out of the labyrinth?

A. by using a ball of thread
B. by using a trail of crumbs
C. by using a bobbing light
D. Hermes tells him the way.

9. Greeks would worship the gods by building temples and:

A. offering human sacrifice.
B. killing Israelites.
C. planting trees.
D. writing and performing plays.

10. The Greek gods are:

A. perfect.
B. all warriors.
C. animals.
D. more like humans, because they were created in man's image and likeness.

CHAPTER 15
The Cradle of Democracy

Perfect Score: 100   Your Score: _____

True or False?

Directions: In the blank beside each statement, write "T" if the statement is *True* or "F" if the statement is *False*. Each correct answer is worth 5 points. 50 possible points.

_____ 1. Greeks were the first people to use democracy as a form of government.

_____ 2. A government where the people govern themselves is called a monarchy.

_____ 3. Draco believed that lenient laws would lead to calmer people.

_____ 4. Solon's laws were wise and helped govern the people more justly.

_____ 5. Solon's laws abolished the practice of Athenians enslaving Athenians.

_____ 6. When their mother couldn't get to the festival, the brothers Cliobus and Bito strapped themselves into her cart and pulled her.

_____ 7. Lycurgus never traveled anywhere and wrote all of Sparta's laws based on his own ideas.

_____ 8. Sparta's army was the strongest and most organized in all of Greece.

_____ 9. Spartan girls were trained to weave and cook while the men trained for battle.

_____ 10. A tyrant is someone who seizes power by force and rules alone.

Multiple Choice

Directions: For each numbered item, circle the letter beside the choice (A, B, C, or D) that best answers the question or completes the statement. Circle only one choice per item. Each correct answer is worth 5 points. 50 possible points.

1. A Greek city-state was called a:

A. province.
B. polis.
C. farms.
D. satrapy.

2. Most ancient governments were:

A. monarchies.
B. oligarchies.
C. democracies.
D. republics.

3. In his laws, a man could be executed for stealing a cabbage.

A. Solon
B. Lycurgus
C. Croesus
D. Draco

4. Solon's laws reduced the power of the rich over the poor by:

A. almsgiving.
B. taxing the rich more.
C. creating an assembly that all could take part in.
D. personally building all the poor new houses.

5. Croesus believed that his possessions brought him:

A. happiness.
B. sorrow.
C. healing.
D. pain.

6. The happiest man Solon ever met was one who had:

A. many wives.
B. many riches.
C. healthy crops.
D. all his days.

7. Those who Solon calls happy are those who:

A. are rich until they die.
B. retain honor until they die.
C. won many wars before they died.
D. grew the largest vegetables for miles before they died.

8. The three things Spartans valued most highly were:

A. war, women, and riches.
B. equality, farms, and art.
C. equality, military power, and simple living.
D. military power, art, and riches.

9. Spartan boys were taken from their families to be trained at the age of:

A. seven.
B. twenty-nine.
C. ten.
D. thirteen.

10. Sparta was unique from other city-states because, though it had democracy, it also had:

A. a king.
B. two kings.
C. a queen.
D. a pope.

CHAPTER 16
The Persian Wars

Perfect Score: 100   Your Score: _____

True or False?

Directions: In the blank beside each statement, write "T" if the statement is *True* or "F" if the statement is *False*. Each correct answer is worth 5 points. 50 possible points.

_____ 1. Xerxes was the first Persian to try to conquer the Greeks.

_____ 2. Xerxes once ordered the water to be punished by whipping.

_____ 3. Athens led the army and the Spartans led the navy in the Persian Wars.

_____ 4. A Spartan king once held off the entire Persian army with only 300 Spartan soldiers.

_____ 5. The Persian's size turned out to be a disadvantage in battling the Greeks.

_____ 6. Themistocles' humility caused him to be praised, and he died happily in Athens.

_____ 7. Athens and Sparta were the two most powerful Greek city-states.

_____ 8. Xerxes believed the Greeks were very powerful opponents.

_____ 9. The Greeks defeated the Persians in wide-open spaces that gave their small armies room to spread out.

_____ 10. The independent city-states all had to unite to defeat Persia.

Multiple Choice

Directions: For each numbered item, circle the letter beside the choice (A, B, C, or D) that best answers the question or completes the statement. Circle only one choice per item. Each correct answer is worth 5 points. 50 possible points.

1. What king went to war against the Greeks in this chapter?

A. Darius
B. Xerxes
C. Cyrus
D. Damian

2. The Greek League was:

A. the miles that the Greeks had to run to escape the Persians.
B. the sports team the Athenians formed to entertain Xerxes.
C. the partnership a Spartan and Athenian formed to bring lawsuits against Persia.
D. an alliance between the Greek city-states to defend Greece against Persia.

3. The Spartan king who held off the entire Persian army with only 300 soldiers at Thermopylae was:

A. Leonidas.
B. Leonardo.
C. Leobald.
D. Leogenes.

4. Themistocles thought the "walls of wood" spoken of by the oracle referred to:

A. the walls of Athens.
B. a shield.
C. ships.
D. spears.

5. The Greeks had a glorious naval victory at the Battle of:

A. Thermopylae.
B. Salamis.
C. Carchemish.
D. Plataea.

6. Who was the Greek general in the battle of Salamis?

A. Aristotle
B. Simeon
C. Themistocles
D. Pollux

7. The Persian Empire was finally defeated at the battle of:

A. Salamis.
B. Thermopylae.
C. Plataea.
D. Appomattox.

8. The general who advised Xerxes and died in Plataea.

A. Mardonius
B. Romulus
C. Cato
D. Leonidas

9. After the Persian wars, the biggest army belonged to:

A. Athens and Thebes.
B. Athens and Sparta.
C. Sparta and Thebes.
D. Sparta and Corinth.

10. Xerxes believed he could defeat the Greeks easily because:

A. they were full of old men.
B. they didn't know how to fight.
C. they were small and disunited.
D. the Spartans refused to help the rest of Greece.

CHAPTER 17
Lovers of Wisdom

Perfect Score: 100   Your Score: _____

True or False?

Directions: In the blank beside each statement, write "T" if the statement is *True* or "F" if the statement is *False*. Each correct answer is worth 5 points. 50 possible points.

_____ 1. In the story, Thales fell into a well.

_____ 2. Thales was a philosopher.

_____ 3. Socrates was happy and willing to die.

_____ 4. Aristotle agreed with everything taught by his master, Plato.

_____ 5. The Greeks were more intellectual than any other ancient people.

_____ 6. Philosophy led to the creation of many sciences.

_____ 7. Socrates taught by asking questions instead of answering them.

_____ 8. Greek philosophers never let their ideas be debated; they considered it an insult.

_____ 9. Greek philosophers would set up schools and teach their ideas.

_____ 10. Many of Aristotle's teachings come to us from the notes taken by his students.

Multiple Choice

Directions: For each numbered item, circle the letter beside the choice (A, B, C, or D) that best answers the question or completes the statement. Circle only one choice per item. Each correct answer is worth 5 points. 50 possible points.

1. A fable is a:

A. short story made up to teach a lesson.
B. fold in a tablecloth.
C. long song or poem recounting heroic deeds.
D. discussion about what the world is made of.

2. "Philosopher" means:

A. finder of truth.
B. asker of questions.
C. lover of wisdom.
D. seeker of life.

3. Greeks loved to argue about:

A. the composition of the world.
B. why we love others.
C. what constitutes justice.
D. all that and more!

4. Pythagoras thought the entire universe was made up of:

A. numbers.
B. water.
C. fire.
D. atoms.

5. Socrates was interested in:

A. the composition of the world.
B. why dogs chase their tails.
C. gravity.
D. how to live a good life.

6. Plato was:

A. Aristotle's student.
B. Diocletian's student.
C. Socrates' student.
D. Thales' student.

7. Aristotle was:

A. Socrates' student.
B. Plato's student.
C. Democritus' student.
D. a character in a fable.

8. Socrates died because:

A. he was a liar.
B. he assassinated an Athenian orator.
C. the rulers were afraid he would turn people against them.
D. he was old.

9. Plato believed that everything in this world is:

A. a copy of perfect ideas.
B. made of fire.
C. true and beautiful.
D. ugly and coarse.

10. Aristotle believed that the soul:

A. is always hungry.
B. doesn't exist.
C. can be corrupted.
D. is the life-force of the body.

CHAPTER 18
Greek Against Greek

Perfect Score: 100   Your Score: _____

True or False?

Directions: In the blank beside each statement, write "T" if the statement is *True* or "F" if the statement is *False*. Each correct answer is worth 5 points. 50 possible points.

_____ 1. Sparta wanted to continue the war against Persia.

_____ 2. Athens wanted to continue the war against Persia.

_____ 3. Athens was kind and just to its allies in the Delian League.

_____ 4. Pericles was a vicious man who oppressed the people.

_____ 5. A "plague" is a large-scale earthquake.

_____ 6. The Peloponnesian War was fought between Athens and Sparta.

_____ 7. Things went badly from the beginning when Athens decided to attack Syracuse.

_____ 8. Sparta was the winner in the Peloponnesian War.

_____ 9. Athens lost the war but kept its independence.

_____ 10. The Peloponnesian War strengthened Greece.

Multiple Choice

Directions: For each numbered item, circle the letter beside the choice (A, B, C, or D) that best answers the question or completes the statement. Circle only one choice per item. Each correct answer is worth 5 points. 50 possible points.

1. The Delian League was:

A. an alliance between Sparta and Athens to attack Persia.
B. an alliance led by Athens against Persia.
C. a Spartan force to attack Persia.
D. an Athenian and Persian alliance to attack Sparta.

2. Some city-states wanted to pull out of the Delian League because:

A. Sparta was friendlier.
B. the Persians were too strong.
C. Athens was becoming an oppressive empire.
D. they had no resources.

3. A king of Sparta who refused to be part of the alliance was:

A. Archidamus.
B. Pericles.
C. Nestor.
D. Herodotus.

4. Pericles built:

A. aqueducts.
B. Zeus' Temple.
C. the Colossus of Rhodes.
D. the Parthenon.

5. Pericles died from:

A. old age.
B. assassination.
C. a plague.
D. drowning.

6. The Spartans went to war with Athens because:

A. Athens was attacking its smaller allies.
B. Athens was getting too powerful.
C. Persia paid them to do it.
D. an oracle told them to.

7. Syracuse was:

A. a brilliant Spartan general.
B. an island allied to Sparta.
C. the prize Athenian warship.
D. the oracle that told of Athenian defeat.

8. The Athenians lost Syracuse because:

A. they foolishly allowed themselves to get trapped in the harbor at the end of fall.
B. their general was arrogant.
C. Apollo put leaks in their boats.
D. traitors burned their ships by night.

9. Nicias:

A. returned to Athens and refused to fight ever again.
B. returned to Athens but was imprisoned.
C. returned to Athens but was killed.
D. died in Syracuse.

10. The Peloponnesian War:

A. reminded the Greeks that they had to stick together to be strong.
B. left Sparta destroyed.
C. weakened Greek unity.
D. drove the Persians out of Greece once and for all.

CHAPTER 19
Alexander the Great

Perfect Score: 100   Your Score: _____

True or False?

Directions: In the blank beside each statement, write "T" if the statement is *True* or "F" if the statement is *False*. Each correct answer is worth 5 points. 50 possible points.

_____ 1. The Spartans were as good at governing as they were at fighting.

_____ 2. The Macedonians were not as intellectual as the Greeks but strong and hardworking.

_____ 3. Philip was impressed when Alexander managed to tame the wild horse.

_____ 4. Alexander was the father of Philip.

_____ 5. Alexander was banished by his own father.

_____ 6. Philip was killed by his wife.

_____ 7. Alexander wanted to make the Persians, Greeks, and Macedonians a single kingdom.

_____ 8. The city of Alexandria is named after Alexander.

_____ 9. Alexander conquered more than any other man before him in history.

_____ 10. Alexander's armies wanted to conquer India, but Alexander was tired and refused.

Multiple Choice

Directions: For each numbered item, circle the letter beside the choice (A, B, C, or D) that best answers the question or completes the statement. Circle only one choice per item. Each correct answer is worth 5 points. 50 possible points.

1. This Greek city-state ended the dominance of Sparta.

A. Athens
B. Thebes
C. Macedonia
D. Persia

2. The king of Macedonia who conquered Greece was:

A. Alexander.
B. Themistocles.
C. Menelaus.
D. Philip.

3. Philip loved the Greeks':

A. fighting skills.
B. architecture.
C. attitude toward life.
D. culture.

4. Alexander's tutor was:

A. Aristotle.
B. Chiron.
C. Friar Benjamin.
D. St. Augustine.

5. When he was young, Alexander performed which amazing feat?

A. He won a battle with a wooden sword.
B. He walked backward up a wall.
C. He tamed a wild horse.
D. He memorized the entire Old Testament.

6. The last Persian king who was defeated by Alexander was:

A. Xerxes II.
B. Dastard IV.
C. Darius III.
D. Kingsley I.

7. A phalanx is:

A. an armored horse.
B. soldiers in a square with long spears.
C. poisoned wine used for assassination.
D. a spiked plank used for boarding enemy ships.

8. One of Alexander's shortcomings was:

A. waiting too long to act.
B. getting drunk and acting rashly.
C. killing people who annoyed him.
D. eating too much and getting fat.

9. Alexander died in:

A. Babylon.
B. Athens.
C. Macedonia.
D. Alexandria.

10. One of the most important things Alexander did was:

A. split his empire into pieces.
B. care for his family above everyone else.
C. provide for the poor in his kingdom.
D. unite half the world under one kingdom and one culture.

CHAPTER 20
The Hellenistic Age

Perfect Score: 100   Your Score: _____

Matching

Directions: In each blank beside a phrase, write the letter of the term that is described by that phrase. Each item is worth 5 points. 45 possible points.

A. Hellenistic
B. Ptolemy
C. Antigonus
D. Seleucus
E. Alexandria

F. the Pharos Lighthouse
G. Ptolemy Philadelphus
H. scribe
I. the Septuagint

_____ 1. the tallest building in the world at the time, and the first of its kind

_____ 2. Alexander's general who took Asia Minor and Syria for his empire

_____ 3. the capital of Egypt under the Ptolemies

_____ 4. Alexander's general who took control of Egypt

_____ 5. built the library of Alexandria

_____ 6. a term used to describe the culture and ways of the Greeks that spread during and after the time of Alexander

_____ 7. the Greek translation of the Old Testament

_____ 8. a person trained to copy things by hand

_____ 9. Alexander's general who took Mesopotamia, Persia, and India for his empire

True or False?

Directions: In the blank beside each statement, write "T" if the statement is *True* or "F" if the statement is *False*. Each correct answer is worth 5 points. 55 possible points.

_____ 1. Alexander divided the empire before he died.

_____ 2. Alexander was buried in his homeland of Macedonia.

_____ 3. Alexandria was one of the most important cities of the Hellenistic era.

_____ 4. Ptolemy was not Egyptian, but he acted like one.

_____ 5. The library of Alexandria included scrolls from many different cultures and peoples.

_____ 6. The Hellenistic kingdoms rarely ever fought each other.

_____ 7. Ptolemy Philadelphus wanted to make Alexandria a center of learning.

_____ 8. The Hellenistic period was a terrible time for people to live.

_____ 9. Everyone was poorly educated in the Hellenistic era.

_____ 10. Seleucus managed to keep control over India.

_____ 11. The word Septuagint means "seventy."

CHAPTER 21
Greek Science

Perfect Score: 100   Your Score: _____

True or False?

Directions: In the blank beside each statement, write "T" if the statement is *True* or "F" if the statement is *False*. Each correct answer is worth 5 points. 50 possible points.

_____ 1. The Greeks were very curious about how things worked.

_____ 2. Euclid taught in Alexandria during Ptolemy's time.

_____ 3. Eratosthenes calculated the distance around the earth.

_____ 4. Euclid perfectly measured the distance from the earth to the sun.

_____ 5. Archimedes built a heat ray to defend his town.

_____ 6. Archimedes built a giant crane to defend his town.

_____ 7. Archimedes built an automated robot to defend his town.

_____ 8. *Elements* was a book about biology.

_____ 9. Eratosthenes and Archimedes were good friends.

_____ 10. The world owes much of its scientific knowledge to the ancient Greeks.

Multiple Choice

Directions: For each numbered item, circle the letter beside the choice (A, B, C, or D) that best answers the question or completes the statement. Circle only one choice per item. Each correct answer is worth 5 points. 50 possible points.

1. The Greek scientists tried to discover:

A. why the grass was green.
B. the secret of how things worked.
C. why the oceans were salty.
D. what drove men to war.

2. Who wrote the book *Elements?*

A. Euclid
B. Demosthenes
C. Plato
D. Eratosthenes

3. *Elements* is a book about:

A. fire, water, wind, and earth.
B. the natural world.
C. geometry.
D. astronomy.

4. Eratosthenes was:

A. an astronomer.
B. the chief librarian of the library of Alexandria.
C. the author of *Elements.*
D. the king of Egypt.

5. Eratosthenes is known as the father of:

A. astronomy.
B. astrology.
C. geometry.
D. geography.

6. Archimedes was:

A. a mathematician.
B. an astronomer.
C. an inventor.
D. a philosopher.

7. Archimedes is best known for discovering:

A. the phrase "Eureka."
B. bathtubs.
C. telescopes.
D. how objects displace water.

8. Archimedes was killed by:

A. Greeks.
B. Romans.
C. Persians.
D. Arabs.

9. Archimedes' Screw is:

A. a giant screw for mining underground.
B. an ancient trampoline.
C. a device for moving water uphill.
D. a heat ray.

10. The city where many scientists came to teach and study was:

A. Alexandria.
B. Athena.
C. Rhodes.
D. Rome.

CHAPTER 22
The Etruscans

Perfect Score: 100   Your Score: _____

True or False?

Directions: In the blank beside each statement, write "T" if the statement is *True* or "F" if the statement is *False*. Each correct answer is worth 5 points. 50 possible points.

_____ 1. The Etruscans migrated to Italy to escape the Assyrians.

_____ 2. The Etruscans left behind mostly jewelry and buildings.

_____ 3. We have many written records and histories of the Etruscan people.

_____ 4. Italy is shaped like a boot.

_____ 5. Italy is a warm and fertile place—perfect for civilization.

_____ 6. As far as we know, Etruscans were the first people to make use of the arch.

_____ 7. The arch isn't as sturdy as the Greek column.

_____ 8. Etruscans used gladiators long before the Romans.

_____ 9. We do not know where the Etruscans came from.

_____ 10. We know about Etruscan funerals from frescoes on Etruscan tombs.

Matching

Directions: In each blank beside a phrase, write the letter of the term that is described by that phrase. Each item is worth 5 points. 50 possible points.

A. Italy
B. the Po
C. the Apennines
D. the Etruscans
E. arch

F. funerals
G. gladiators
H. Haruspex
I. Rome
J. Latins

_____ 1. men who fight and die for sport and sacrifice

_____ 2. mountain range that runs through Italy

_____ 3. grand, spectacular events in Etruscan culture

_____ 4. people who lived in Italy around 800 B.C.

_____ 5. a priest who looks at dead animal livers to find messages from the gods

_____ 6. boot-shaped country

_____ 7. the small tribe that populated Rome

_____ 8. rounded structure that helps hold up the weight of a building

_____ 9. tiny city ruled by the Etruscans that would one day change the world

_____ 10. river that runs through Italy

CHAPTER 23
The City of Seven Hills

Perfect Score: 100   Your Score: _____

True or False?

Directions: In the blank beside each statement, write "T" if the statement is *True* or "F" if the statement is *False*. Each correct answer is worth 5 points. 50 possible points.

_____ 1. The Romans got wives by stealing women.

_____ 2. In the early republic, laws were unfair to plebeians.

_____ 3. Patricians were the vast majority of Rome in the old republic.

_____ 4. The plebeians left Rome until laws would be made that protected them.

_____ 5. The tribune represented the plebeians' interests.

_____ 6. Rome was almost always at peace.

_____ 7. Rome was sacked in 390 B.C. by barbarians.

_____ 8. Rome almost always lost her wars.

_____ 9. Rome was good at war but bad at governing.

_____ 10. Rome was ruled by kings before the overthrow of the Tarquins.

Multiple Choice

Directions: For each numbered item, circle the letter beside the choice (A, B, C, or D) that best answers the question or completes the statement. Circle only one choice per item. Each correct answer is worth 5 points. 50 possible points.

1. The river Rome is founded by is the:

A. Rubicon.
B. Tiber.
C. Po.
D. Amazon.

2. According to legend, Rome was founded by:

A. Remus.
B. Julius Caesar.
C. Cicero.
D. Romulus.

3. The traditional year for the founding of Rome.

A. 1700 B.C.
B. 500 B.C.
C. 50 B.C.
D. 753 B.C.

4. The Etruscan family that took power over Rome was the:

A. Tarquins.
B. Castors.
C. Clytemnestras.
D. Amarants.

5. A republic is a government system where:

A. the people elect a king.
B. the people elect officials to make laws.
C. a dictator selects officials under him.
D. the people elect an emperor.

6. Instead of a king, the Roman republic had:

A. two kings.
B. two consuls.
C. one consul.
D. one emperor.

7. Roman laws were made by:

A. a committee.
B. the emperor.
C. the Senate.
D. one of the kings.

8. Aediles are:

A. lower officials to maintain waterways and roads.
B. lower officials to collect taxes.
C. higher officials to declare war.
D. higher officials to elect consuls.

9. Patricians were:

A. servants of the Roman people.
B. poor families in Rome.
C. the pets of the Roman people.
D. the oldest and richest families in Rome.

10. Plebeians were:

A. poor families in Rome.
B. the oldest and riches families in Rome.
C. sick people in Rome.
D. the soldiers of the Roman army.

CHAPTER 24
The Punic Wars

Perfect Score: 100   Your Score: _____

Matching

Directions: In each blank beside a phrase, write the letter of the term that is described by that phrase. Each item is worth 5 points. 55 possible points.

A. Carthage
B. Phoenicians
C. Sicily
D. Punici
E. Hamilcar
F. Hannibal

G. mercenary
H. Alps
I. Gaius Flaminius
J. Lake Trasimene
K. Cornelius Scipio

_____ 1. Roman name for the Carthaginians

_____ 2. soldier who fights for whoever pays him

_____ 3. Carthaginian general in the First Punic War

_____ 4. founders of Carthage

_____ 5. Roman consul who led the army in Second Punic War and lost a battle

_____ 6. city-state in Africa, right across the sea from Italy

_____ 7. disastrous battle where Hannibal soundly defeated the Romans

_____ 8. the mountain range crossed by Hannibal and his army into Italy

_____ 9. island fought over by Carthage and Rome

_____10. brilliant Carthaginian general of the Second Punic War

_____11. Roman general who invaded Africa to attack Carthage

True or False?

Directions: In the blank beside each statement, write "T" if the statement is *True* or "F" if the statement is *False*. Each correct answer is worth 5 points. 45 possible points.

_____ 1. The battle of Cannae was a Roman victory.

_____ 2. Instead of attacking Rome, Hannibal dawdled and waited for extra help from Carthage.

_____ 3. At the battle of Zama, Rome won.

_____ 4. Hannibal was executed by Rome.

_____ 5. Carthage brought the Third Punic War upon itself by violating their peace terms.

_____ 6. Scipio Africanus fought the Third Punic War with Carthage.

_____ 7. Carthage was burned to the ground after the Third Punic War.

_____ 8. After the Punic wars, Rome truly became an empire.

_____ 9. Rome lost the First Punic War.

CHAPTER 25
Greece and Rome Collide

Perfect Score: 100   Your Score: _____

True or False?

Directions: In the blank beside each statement, write "T" if the statement is *True* or "F" if the statement is *False*. Each correct answer is worth 5 points. 50 possible points.

_____ 1. Romans thought Greek culture was very dull.

_____ 2. Rome and Greece have the same gods but with different names.

_____ 3. The Romans adopted Greek culture.

_____ 4. Egypt hated Rome and wanted to make war against it.

_____ 5. Egypt allied with Rome to defeat Antiochus III.

_____ 6. Antiochus III lost the war with Rome and much of his land.

_____ 7. Antiochus IV Epiphanes took out his loss against Rome on the Jews.

_____ 8. Rome had an alliance with the Maccabees.

_____ 9. The Maccabees won independence from the Seleucids.

_____ 10. Antiochus finally captured and killed Judas Maccabeus.

Multiple Choice

Directions: For each numbered item, circle the letter beside the choice (A, B, C, or D) that best answers the question or completes the statement. Circle only one choice per item. Each correct answer is worth 5 points. 50 possible points.

1. The king of Macedonia who was beaten by Rome.

A. Alexander
B. Aristotle
C. Phillip V
D. Darius III

2. A maniple is a:

A. square of 120 soldiers.
B. powerful crossbow.
C. poison dart.
D. traitor.

3. A legion is:

A. a huge bridge.
B. 30 maniples.
C. a Macedonian fighting technique.
D. highly trained guards.

4. The Greek city-states were:

A. happy to be rid of the Macedonians but didn't want to be ruled by Rome.
B. sad to be rid of the Macedonians.
C. happy to be rid of the Macedonians and happy to be ruled by Rome.
D. just looking for somebody to love them.

5. Antiochus III was:

A. the king of Egypt.
B. the king of Greece.
C. the king of the Seleucid empire.
D. the ruler of Carthage.

6. He tried to invade Egypt but was prevented by Gaius Popillius Laenas.

A. Antiochus IV Epiphanes
B. Antiochus III
C. Hannibal II
D. Gaius Cornelius

7. Mattathias was:

A. an old Jewish man who refused to sacrifice a pig to Zeus.
B. a great warrior who killed many Romans.
C. a girl who dressed as a boy in order to join the army.
D. a crown prince who was killed by Antiochus IV.

8. "Maccabeus" means:

A. he who kills many men.
B. he who flies like a bee.
C. the hammer.
D. war machine.

9. In 164 B.C., Judas Maccabeus and his brothers:

A. assassinated Antiochus IV.
B. began the Jewish rebellion.
C. made an alliance with Rome.
D. threw the Greek idols out of the Temple and rededicated it to God.

10. Two books of the Bible are dedicated to the story of:

A. Rome.
B. the Maccabees.
C. Antiochus IV's failures.
D. Ptolemaic Egyptian politics.

CHAPTER 26
Marius and Sulla

Perfect Score: 100   Your Score: _____

True or False?

Directions: In the blank beside each statement, write "T" if the statement is *True* or "F" if the statement is *False*. Each correct answer is worth 5 points. 50 possible points.

_____ 1. Roman soldiers often lost their farms.

_____ 2. Many people moved to the city of Rome because the rich owned the countryside.

_____ 3. The Land Bill would have given land back to the poor people of Rome.

_____ 4. Wealthy senators thought Tiberius Gracchus didn't have enough power and should seek more.

_____ 5. Tiberius was killed by his brother.

_____ 6. Gaius Gracchus killed himself after losing a battle.

_____ 7. Marius served as consul seven times.

_____ 8. Sulla took Rome but left soon after to fight a different war.

_____ 9. Sulla was nicknamed "Felix" because he was very sad.

_____ 10. After the civil wars, the Roman republic was stronger than ever.

Multiple Choice

Directions: For each numbered item, circle the letter beside the choice (A, B, C, or D) that best answers the question or completes the statement. Circle only one choice per item. Each correct answer is worth 5 points. 50 possible points.

1. Latifundia were:

A. Roman markets.
B. huge farms worked by slaves.
C. herds of cows and donkeys.
D. Roman marriages.

2. Tiberius Gracchus was:

A. a general who gave up his farm for a poor family.
B. the god of agriculture.
C. the tribune who proposed the Land Bill.
D. a donkey who pulled a cart of sick people ten miles to get medicine from Rome.

3. Populares were:

A. people who supported the Land Bill.
B. popular stage performers.
C. high priests of Minerva.
D. criminals against Rome.

4. Optimates were:

A. people who opposed the Land Bill.
B. high-class businessmen.
C. high priests of Apollo.
D. criminals against Rome.

5. Gaius Gracchus was:

A. Tiberius' brother who killed him.
B. Tiberius' son who replaced him.
C. Tiberius' brother who replaced him.
D. Tiberius' son who killed him.

6. Gaius Marius was:

A. an important Populare and general.
B. an important Optimate and general.
C. a farmer killed for his land.
D. the first Roman emperor.

7. One of Marius' major reforms was:

A. the city architecture.
B. the farmland.
C. the laws.
D. the army.

8. Cornelius Sulla was:

A. an important Populare general.
B. an important Optimate general.
C. a farmer killed for his land.
D. the first Roman emperor.

9. A civil war is:

A. a war between nations.
B. a war fought with no weapons.
C. a war between rich people and poor people.
D. a war where a country fights itself.

10. A dictator is:

A. a teacher.
B. a man who relates stories by word of mouth.
C. an office that allowed one man extraordinary power.
D. the man with the real power behind the throne.

CHAPTER 27
The Rise and Fall of Julius Caesar

Perfect Score: 100   Your Score: _____

True or False?

Directions: In the blank beside each statement, write "T" if the statement is *True* or "F" if the statement is *False*. Each correct answer is worth 5 points. 50 possible points.

_____ 1. Pompey was a great general.

_____ 2. Caesar was a great general.

_____ 3. Caesar rejoiced when Pompey was killed.

_____ 4. Caesar conquered Gaul and invaded Britain.

_____ 5. Caesar was a very unforgiving man.

_____ 6. Caesar cared mostly about power and little else.

_____ 7. Caesar appointed himself dictator for life.

_____ 8. The people rejoiced at Caesar's assassination.

_____ 9. A *will* is something people write to tell how they want their property distributed after their death.

_____ 10. Octavian was the first Roman emperor.

Matching

Directions: In each blank beside a phrase, write the letter of the term that is described by that phrase. Each item is worth 5 points. 50 possible points.

A. Pompey
B. triumph
C. Julius Caesar
D. Ptolemy XIII
E. Cleopatra

F. Marc Antony
G. Brutus
H. Octavian
I. Actium
J. *Princeps, Augustus*

_____ 1. king of Egypt who killed Pompey

_____ 2. conspirator who helped to kill Caesar

_____ 3. Egyptian queen who Caesar fell in love with

_____ 4. Caesar's most trusted friend

_____ 5. leader of the Optimates; a great general who did away with the Seleucid empire

_____ 6. Caesar's nephew and heir to his legacy

_____ 7. First Citizen, Revered One

_____ 8. leader of the Populares, spared by Sulla, and had "the spirit of Marius"

_____ 9. a massive parade for conquering generals

_____ 10. battle where Octavian defeated Antony and Cleopatra

CHAPTER 28
The Coming of Christ

Perfect Score: 100

Your Score: _____

True or False?

Directions: In the blank beside each statement, write "T" if the statement is *True* or "F" if the statement is *False*. Each correct answer is worth 5 points. 50 possible points.

_____ 1. Romans thought happiness consisted of wealth and power.

_____ 2. The Incarnation is the most important event in the history of the world.

_____ 3. Joseph was descended from King David.

_____ 4. Mary was born without sin.

_____ 5. Jesus only preached and never acted.

_____ 6. Jesus wanted rich apostles so that they would give money to the poor.

_____ 7. Jesus said, "I did not come to serve, but to be served."

_____ 8. The group that hated Jesus the most was called the Pharisees.

_____ 9. In the Eucharist, the bread and wine become the Body and Blood of Jesus.

_____ 10. Pontius Pilate was convinced of Jesus' guilt and therefore had him crucified.

Multiple Choice

Directions: For each numbered item, circle the letter beside the choice (A, B, C, or D) that best answers the question or completes the statement. Circle only one choice per item. Each correct answer is worth 5 points. 50 possible points.

1. What is the Incarnation?

A. when Joseph married Mary
B. when Mary was born
C. when God became man
D. when Jesus was presented in the temple

2. What does "B.C." stand for?

A. Before Christ
B. Before Calvin
C. Bona Christa
D. Bellum Christos

3. What does "A.D." stand for?

A. After Domitian
B. After Dominion
C. Anno Domini
D. Alexander's Death

4. What does "Christ" mean in Greek?

A. God is with us
B. father
C. love conquers all
D. messiah

5. Where did Jesus begin His ministry?

A. Jerusalem
B. Galilee
C. Rome
D. Nazareth

6. What does "Apostle" mean in Greek?

A. follower
B. messenger
C. warrior
D. priest

7. What is the Eucharist?

A. Communion
B. the Last Supper
C. bread and wine becoming the Body and Blood of Jesus
D. a body of priests

8. Who betrayed Jesus?

A. Peter
B. Paul
C. Jude
D. Judas

9. What does Golgotha mean?

A. place of the skull
B. hill of the cross
C. criminals must die
D. Jesus has saved us

10. The traditional date of Jesus' death is:

A. 30 A.D.
B. 33 A.D.
C. 25 A.D.
D. 20 A.D.

CHAPTER 29
Fishers of Men

Perfect Score: 100   Your Score: _____

True or False?

Directions: In the blank beside each statement, write "T" if the statement is *True* or "F" if the statement is *False*. Each correct answer is worth 5 points. 50 possible points.

_____ 1. St. Paul used to hate Christians and tried to kill them.

_____ 2. St. Paul was one of the original twelve apostles.

_____ 3. St. Paul replaced Judas as one of the twelve.

_____ 4. Most apostles preached among Jews, but Paul preached among Gentiles.

_____ 5. St. Peter said Christians had to follow Mosaic Law.

_____ 6. Jesus called all people to His Church, not just Jews.

_____ 7. Deacons were ordained to help distribute to the poor and help the sick.

_____ 8. By the time the last apostle died, there were almost no churches anywhere.

_____ 9. St. Peter was the leader of the apostles.

_____ 10. St. Paul believed that only Jews should be allowed to convert to Christianity.

Multiple Choice

Directions: For each numbered item, circle the letter beside the choice (A, B, C, or D) that best answers the question or completes the statement. Circle only one choice per item. Each correct answer is worth 5 points. 50 possible points.

1. Who were the first to realize that Jesus Christ had risen from the dead?

A. the Apostles
B. the Pharisees
C. several women, including Mary Magdalen
D. Pilate and his household

2. What was the day called when the Holy Spirit descended on the Apostles?

A. Pentecost
B. the Ascension
C. the Assumption
D. the Immaculate Conception

3. Who is the Pope?

A. a bishop who becomes a saint
B. leader of the Catholic Church; Peter's successor
C. any male saint
D. a Doctor of the Church

4. What does "Christian" mean?

A. followers of Christ
B. Christ-like
C. Christmas lovers
D. fishers of men

5. Where did Jesus appear to Paul?

A. the road to Emmaus
B. the road to Jerusalem
C. the road to Galilee
D. the road to Damascus

6. Why was a council called in Jerusalem?

A. to determine if Christians had to be circumcised
B. to determine if Christians had to follow the Law of Moses
C. to determine if Gentiles were allowed to convert to Christianity
D. to determine if Roman soldiers were allowed to be Christians

7. "Catholic" means:

A. almost Christians.
B. apostolic.
C. holy.
D. universal.

8. What is a martyr?

A. someone who dies for the sake of Jesus
B. someone who dies for his family
C. someone who dies while praying
D. someone who rises from the dead

9. What is a bishop?

A. the successor of Peter
B. a male saint
C. chief pastor of a particular church
D. a priest who is martyred

10. What is another word for priest?

A. bishop
B. deacon
C. presbyter
D. protestant

CHAPTER 30
Life Under the Julio-Claudians

Perfect Score: 100   Your Score: _____

True or False?

Directions: In the blank beside each statement, write "T" if the statement is *True* or "F" if the statement is *False*. Each correct answer is worth 5 points. 50 possible points.

_____ 1. After Augustus, Rome again became a republic.

_____ 2. Augustus built many grand buildings throughout Rome.

_____ 3. Caligula pretended to be insane but was actually very smart.

_____ 4. Imperator means "He who holds power."

_____ 5. Jesus was crucified during Tiberius' reign.

_____ 6. Augustus' family was just as good at ruling as he was.

_____ 7. Nero killed both St. Peter and St. Paul in his persecutions.

_____ 8. St. Peter was crucified upside down.

_____ 9. St. Paul was crucified upside down.

_____ 10. Nero was the last of the Julio-Claudians.

Matching

Directions: In each blank beside a phrase, write the letter of the term that is described by that phrase. Each item is worth 5 points. 50 possible points.

A. Tiberius
B. Caligula
C. Claudius
D. Agrippina
E. Nero

F. the Great Fire
G. villa
H. Insulae
I. Triclinium
J. clients and patrons

_____ 1. a country farm

_____ 2. Tiberius' grand-nephew, who was insane

_____ 3. devastating event in Rome blamed on the Christians

_____ 4. Augustus' stepson, a cruel emperor

_____ 5. terrible emperor who persecuted Christians

_____ 6. city apartments where common people lived

_____ 7. Nero's mother, a violent woman who killed Claudius

_____ 8. two groups of people who depended on each other in Roman society

_____ 9. the dining room

_____ 10. Caligula's uncle, a decent emperor who once hid behind a curtain

CHAPTER 31
Five "Good" Emperors

Perfect Score: 100   Your Score: _____

Matching

Directions: In each blank beside a phrase, write the letter of the term that is described by that phrase. Each item is worth 5 points. 50 possible points.

A. Galba
B. Vespasian
C. colosseum
D. Titus
E. Domitian

F. Nerva
G. Trajan
H. Hadrian
I. Antoninus Pius
J. Marcus Aurelius

_____ 1. Nerva's successor; a popular Spanish general

_____ 2. kind-hearted emperor who built the colosseum

_____ 3. first of the "good emperors"; sickly man who died soon after election

_____ 4. the man who revolted against Nero

_____ 5. massive structure used for chariot races and gladiatorial combat

_____ 6. Vespasian's son who became emperor and was killed

_____ 7. emperor who built a wall to border Rome's lands

_____ 8. Vespasian's son who conquered Jerusalem

_____ 9. emperor who spent his reign fighting barbarians

_____ 10. emperor with the most peaceful reign

True or False?

Directions: In the blank beside each statement, write "T" if the statement is *True* or "F" if the statement is *False*. Each correct answer is worth 5 points. 50 possible points.

_____ 1. A barbarian was someone from outside the empire who didn't have Roman culture.

_____ 2. The five good emperors had the longest time of peace and stability Rome ever knew.

_____ 3. The five emperors were all very tolerant of Christians.

_____ 4. Commodus is known as "the sixth good emperor."

_____ 5. By the time Commodus died, the empire was again in chaos.

_____ 6. The Jews successfully revolted against Vespasian and Rome.

_____ 7. The Senate chose the first of the five good emperors.

_____ 8. All of the five good emperors were related.

_____ 9. These emperors are called "good" because they brought prosperity and peace to Rome.

_____ 10. The "good emperors" persecuted Christians.

CHAPTER 32
Collapse

Perfect Score: 100   Your Score: _____

True or False?

Directions: In the blank beside each statement, write "T" if the statement is *True* or "F" if the statement is *False*. Each correct answer is worth 5 points. 50 possible points.

_____ 1. Septimius Severus reigned for eighteen years and reformed the military.

_____ 2. Thanks to the civil disunity, barbarians began to invade Roman lands.

_____ 3. Persia wanted to attack Rome but was too weak.

_____ 4. Christians were often blamed for Rome's troubles.

_____ 5. The persecutions stopped the spread of Christianity.

_____ 6. Aurelian was a good and capable emperor.

_____ 7. Aurelian took back all the lands Zenobia and Postumus had taken.

_____ 8. Aurelian tried to conquer Persia and succeeded.

_____ 9. Christians were some of the most honest and hardworking Roman citizens.

_____ 10. The loss of farmland to barbarians was not a big deal.

Multiple Choice

Directions: For each numbered item, circle the letter beside the choice (A, B, C, or D) that best answers the question or completes the statement. Circle only one choice per item. Each correct answer is worth 5 points. 50 possible points.

1. The most important support an emperor needed came from the:

A. senators.
B. people.
C. army.
D. consuls.

2. Two emperors who persecuted Christians were:

A. Commodus and Marcus Aurelius.
B. Gaius and Phillipus.
C. Flavius and Cornelius.
D. Decius and Valerian.

3. The woman who broke Egypt, Syria, and Palestine away from Rome was:

A. Zenobia.
B. Cleopatra II.
C. Postumus.
D. Aurelia Cornelii.

4. Aurelian did this as an act of defense.

A. tripled the size of the army
B. built huge walls around the city of Rome
C. exiled all of his enemies
D. killed anyone who looked like a barbarian

5. Sol Invictus means:

A. lonely survivor.
B. sole conqueror.
C. unconquerable sun.
D. sun of victory.

6. Two famous people killed during the Christian persecutions of this time were:

A. Felicity and Perpetua.
B. Cornelius and Cyprian.
C. Cosmos and Damien.
D. Peter and Paul.

7. One of the main barbarian tribes was the:

A. Vandals.
B. Hippies.
C. Collerics.
D. Heimlichs.

8. Because of the barbarians:

A. ships couldn't leave port.
B. money became scarce and trade became difficult.
C. Rome was burned to the ground.
D. there was a lack of horses for cavalry.

9. From 235–285 A.D., Rome had:

A. peace and prosperity.
B. more parties than at any other period.
C. a terrible plague.
D. over 50 emperors.

10. Almost all emperors in this period:

A. committed suicide.
B. died of plague.
C. were murdered.
D. lived long and prospered.

CHAPTER 33
The Growth of the Catholic Church

Perfect Score: 100   Your Score: _____

True or False?

Directions: In the blank beside each statement, write "T" if the statement is *True* or "F" if the statement is *False*. Each correct answer is worth 5 points. 50 possible points.

_____ 1. The Romans accused Christians of many things they did not do.

_____ 2. Romans thought Christians were cannibals.

_____ 3. Some Christians wrote letters to say they were sorry for their behavior.

_____ 4. St. Justin Martyr wrote about the Masses of the early church.

_____ 5. St. Justin Martyr was never actually martyred.

_____ 6. Theologians studied and wrote about philosophy.

_____ 7. Catholics never disagreed about theology.

_____ 8. Heretics denied the teachings of the Church and taught others to do the same.

_____ 9. Priests, more than bishops, were the backbone of the Church.

_____ 10. By the time of St. Cyprian's death, Christians were the majority of the Roman Empire.

Multiple Choice

Directions: For each numbered item, circle the letter beside the choice (A, B, C, or D) that best answers the question or completes the statement. Circle only one choice per item. Each correct answer is worth 5 points. 50 possible points.

1. What was the Catholic Church compared to at this time?

A. an old tree
B. a young tree
C. a rose
D. a lily

2. An apologist is:

A. someone always saying they are sorry.
B. a murderer of Christians.
C. a writer who explained Christianity to pagans.
D. an intelligent mathematician.

3. Who is the first and greatest apologist?

A. St. Justin Martyr
B. St. Ignatius of Antioch
C. St. Cyprian
D. St. Flavia

4. What is theology?

A. the question of why things are the way they are
B. the study of the natural world
C. the study of God and His revelation
D. the pursuit of happiness

5. What is a synod?

A. bishops from an area gathering to discuss theology and discipline
B. a Roman soldier who converts to Christianity
C. a Catholic who falls away during persecution but then returns
D. more than ten Christians being martyred at once

6. The Bishop of which city was the most important?

A. Antioch
B. Jerusalem
C. Alexandria
D. Rome

7. What does "heresy" mean?

A. unnaturally hairy
B. sick for a long period of time
C. confused in the mind
D. wrong thinking

8. Where was St. Cyprian bishop?

A. Rome
B. Carthage
C. Alexandria
D. Antioch

9. The Donatist heresy taught that:

A. some sins couldn't be forgiven.
B. you shouldn't give to the poor.
C. Christ was not the Son of God.
D. giving to the Church was optional.

10. Gnostics taught that:

A. all insects were evil.
B. all matter was evil.
C. wisdom was unnecessary.
D. truth was relative.

CHAPTER 34
The Empire Divided

Perfect Score: 100   Your Score: _____

True or False?

Directions: In the blank beside each statement, write "T" if the statement is *True* or "F" if the statement is *False*. Each correct answer is worth 5 points. 50 possible points.

_____ 1. Diocletian came from a humble background.

_____ 2. Diocletian split the empire up into different parts.

_____ 3. Diocletian and Maximian both chose successors while alive.

_____ 4. Diocletian had always hated Christians.

_____ 5. Diocletian and Galerius blamed the palace fire on angry gods.

_____ 6. The Decree of Persecution was enforced the same everywhere.

_____ 7. Diocletian was a complete success besides the persecution.

_____ 8. Diocletian was the first emperor to voluntarily leave office.

_____ 9. Martyrs were both men and women.

_____ 10. Diocletian and Maximian were both killed.

Matching

Directions: In each blank beside a phrase, write the letter of the term that is described by that phrase. Each item is worth 5 points. 50 possible points.

A. Diocletian
B. Maximian
C. Galerius
D. Romanus
E. the Great Persecution

F. Decree of Persecution
G. Constantius Chlorus
H. Sebastian
I. Agnes
J. Succession Plan

_____ 1. Diocletian's successor who hated Christians

_____ 2. law that destroyed churches, Bibles, and exiled or killed all Christians who resisted

_____ 3. famous martyr who survived being shot by many arrows

_____ 4. emperor who divided the empire

_____ 5. deacon who angered Diocletian and was executed

_____ 6. an attempt to keep Rome from civil war by choosing successors while alive

_____ 7. ruler of the western part of the empire

_____ 8. famous martyr who refused to marry in order to remain a virgin

_____ 9. Maximian's successor; ignored the Decree of Persecution

_____ 10. most terrible time of all that Christians had endured

CHAPTER 35
In This Sign, Conquer

Perfect Score: 100   Your Score: _____

True or False?

Directions: In the blank beside each statement, write "T" if the statement is *True* or "F" if the statement is *False*. Each correct answer is worth 5 points. 50 possible points.

_____ 1. Diocletian farmed cabbages in his retirement.

_____ 2. Diocletian's plan to keep the empire from civil war succeeded.

_____ 3. Constantine was hesitant to attack Rome since it was so well fortified.

_____ 4. God sent Constantine a dream telling him to have his men paint Christian symbols on their shields.

_____ 5. Constantine refused to sacrifice to Jupiter.

_____ 6. St. Peter's basilica was built where the circus of Nero had once been.

_____ 7. Constantine gave much money to build churches for Christians.

_____ 8. When Constantine became emperor, Christianity was the majority religion in the empire.

_____ 9. Constantine's reign marks the beginning of the end of the pagan world.

_____ 10. Constantine never actually converted to Christianity.

Multiple Choice

Directions: For each numbered item, circle the letter beside the choice (A, B, C, or D) that best answers the question or completes the statement. Circle only one choice per item. Each correct answer is worth 5 points. 50 possible points.

1. Constantius' son was:

A. Constantine.
B. Constance.
C. Constantius II.
D. Chlorus.

2. The man ruling Italy at the time of Constantine was:

A. Maximian.
B. Maxentius.
C. Maxwell.
D. Max.

3. Constantine and his army crossed the Alps, just like which other general?

A. Maximian
B. Julius Caesar
C. Augustine
D. Hannibal

4. What does "In hoc signo vinces" mean?

A. In this sign, conquer.
B. Vanquish in the city.
C. Victory upon the morn.
D. In victory, there is God.

5. The letter X and the letter P are the first two letters of what in Greek?

A. cross
B. victory
C. Christians
D. Christ

6. What was the Edict of Milan?

A. persecuted pagans
B. legalized Christianity
C. forgave Constantine's enemies
D. made Christianity the one and only religion of Rome

7. When was the Edict of Milan issued?

A. 300
B. 310
C. 313
D. 330

8. Where did Constantine see "*In hoc signo vinces*"?

A. on a hill
B. on a cross
C. by a church
D. in a dream

9. Maxentius was:

A. an usurper.
B. the rightful successor.
C. the son of Diocletian.
D. the brother of Galerius.

10. What is civilization built on Christianity called?

A. Catholic world
B. Paganism
C. Christendom
D. earth for Jesus

Answer Key

CHAPTER 1 – The Dawn of Civilization
Test Book pages 1–3

True or False?
1. F   2. T   3. T   4. T   5. F   6. T   7. F   8. T   9. T   10. F

Multiple Choice
1. C   2. A   3. D   4. B   5. C   6. B   7. D   8. A   9. D   10. C

CHAPTER 2 – The Gift of the Nile
Test Book pages 5–7

Matching
1. J   2. C   3. B   4. H   5. G   6. I   7. A   8. D   9. F   10. E   11. L   12. K

Multiple Choice
1. A   2. D   3. B   4. B   5. C   6. D   7. D   8. B

CHAPTER 3 – Egypt in the Pyramid Age
Test Book pages 9–11

True or False?
1. T   2. F   3. T   4. T   5. F

Multiple Choice
1. B   2. C   3. D   4. A   5. D   6. A   7. A   8. B   9. D   10. D   11. B   12. A
13. D   14. C   15. B

CHAPTER 4 – The Land Between Two Rivers
Test Book pages 13–15

True or False?
1. T   2. F   3. T   4. F   5. T   6. T   7. T   8. F   9. T   10. F

Multiple Choice
1. C   2. D   3. B   4. C   5. A   6. D   7. B   8. C   9. A   10. D

CHAPTER 5 – Egyptian Empires
Test Book pages 17–19

Matching
1. D   2. G   3. A   4. J   5. B   6. C   7. E   8. I   9. F   10. H

Multiple Choice
1. C   2. A   3. D   4. D   5. B   6. C   7. A   8. D   9. B   10. A

CHAPTER 6 – Peoples of the Levant
Test Book pages 21–22

True or False?
1. T   2. T   3. F   4. F   5. T   6. T   7. F   8. T   9. T   10. F   11. T   12. F
13. T   14. F   15. F

Multiple Choice
1. D   2. A   3. B   4. C   5. B

CHAPTER 7 – The God of Israel
Test Book pages 23–26

Multiple Choice
1. B   2. D   3. A   4. A   5. C   6. B   7. D   8. B   9. A   10. C   11. B   12. D
13. C   14. A   15. D   16. D   17. A   18. D   19. B   20. C

CHAPTER 8 – The Kingdom of David
Test Book pages 27–28

True or False?
1. T   2. F   3. T   4. F   5. T   6. T   7. T   8. F   9. F   10. T

Matching
1. G   2. B   3. C   4. A   5. F   6. I   7. H   8. D   9. E   10. O   11. K   12. M
13. N   14. J   15. L

CHAPTER 9 – The Bearded Kings of the North
Test Book pages 29–31

True or False?
1. T   2. T   3. F   4. F   5. F   6. T   7. F   8. T   9. T   10. F

Multiple Choice
1. B   2. C   3. A   4. B   5. C   6. D   7. B   8. A   9. B   10. D

CHAPTER 10 – The Splendor of Babylon
Test Book pages 33–35

True or False?
1. F   2. F   3. T   4. T   5. T

Matching
1. C   2. A   3. G   4. B   5. J   6. H   7. E   8. D   9. I   10. F

Multiple Choice
1. C   2. B   3. C   4. A   5. D   6. B   7. A   8. D   9. C   10. D

CHAPTER 11 – The Rise of Persia
Test Book pages 37–39

True or False?
1. T   2. T   3. F   4. F   5. F   6. T   7. T   8. F   9. T   10. T

Multiple Choice
1. B   2. A   3. B   4. D   5. C   6. A   7. B   8. A   9. C   10. D

CHAPTER 12 – People of the Isles
Test Book pages 41–42

Matching
1. C   2. F   3. B   4. J   5. A   6. H   7. D   8. I   9. G   10. E

True or False?
1. T   2. F   3. F   4. F   5. F   6. T   7. F   8. F   9. T   10. T

CHAPTER 13 – The Founding of Greece
Test Book pages 43–45

Multiple Choice
1. A   2. C   3. B   4. D   5. C   6. B   7. A   8. B   9. D   10. C

True or False?
1. F   2. T   3. F   4. T   5. T   6. T   7. T   8. T   9. F   10. F

CHAPTER 14 – Greek Mythology
Test Book pages 47–49

Matching
1. C   2. E   3. I   4. G   5. J   6. A   7. B   8. D   9. F   10. H

Multiple Choice
1. D   2. B   3. A   4. A   5. C   6. B   7. C   8. A   9. D   10. D

CHAPTER 15 – The Cradle of Democracy
Test Book pages 51–53

True or False?
1. T   2. F   3. F   4. T   5. T   6. T   7. F   8. T   9. F   10. T

Multiple Choice
1. B   2. A   3. D   4. C   5. A   6. D   7. B   8. C   9. A   10. B

CHAPTER 16 – The Persian Wars
Test Book pages 55–57

True or False?
1. F   2. T   3. F   4. T   5. T   6. F   7. T   8. F   9. F   10. F

Multiple Choice
1. B   2. D   3. A   4. C   5. B   6. C   7. C   8. A   9. B   10. C

CHAPTER 17 – Lovers of Wisdom
Test Book pages 59–61

True or False?
1. T   2. T   3. T   4. F   5. T   6. T   7. T   8. F   9. T   10. T

Multiple Choice
1. A   2. C   3. D   4. A   5. D   6. C   7. B   8. C   9. A   10. D

CHAPTER 18 – Greek Against Greek
Test Book pages 63–65

True or False?
1. F   2. T   3. F   4. F   5. F   6. T   7. T   8. T   9. F   10. F

Multiple Choice
1. B   2. C   3. A   4. D   5. C   6. A   7. B   8. A   9. D   10. C

CHAPTER 19 – Alexander the Great
Test Book pages 67–69

True or False?
1. F   2. T   3. T   4. F   5. T   6. F   7. T   8. T   9. T   10. F

Multiple Choice
1. B   2. D   3. D   4. A   5. C   6. C   7. B   8. B   9. A   10. D

CHAPTER 20 – The Hellenistic Age
Test Book pages 71–72

Matching
1. F   2. C   3. E   4. B   5. G   6. A   7. I   8. H   9. D

True or False?
1. F   2. F   3. T   4. T   5. T   6. F   7. T   8. F   9. F   10. F   11. T

CHAPTER 21 – Greek Science
Test Book pages 73–75

True or False?
1. T   2. T   3. T   4. F   5. T   6. T   7. F   8. F   9. T   10. T

Multiple Choice
1. B   2. A   3. C   4. B   5. D   6. C   7. D   8. B   9. C   10. A

CHAPTER 22 – The Etruscans
Test Book pages 77–78

True or False?
1. F   2. T   3. F   4. T   5. T   6. T   7. F   8. T   9. T   10. T

Matching
1. G   2. C   3. F   4. D   5. H   6. A   7. J   8. E   9. I   10. B

CHAPTER 23 – The City of Seven Hills
Test Book pages 79–81

True or False?
1. T   2. T   3. F   4. T   5. T   6. F   7. T   8. F   9. F   10. T

Multiple Choice
1. B   2. D   3. D   4. A   5. B   6. B   7. C   8. A   9. D   10. A

CHAPTER 24 – The Punic Wars
Test Book pages 83–84

Matching
1. D   2. G   3. E   4. B   5. I   6. A   7. J   8. H   9. C   10. F   11. K

True or False?
1. F   2. T   3. T   4. F   5. T   6. F   7. T   8. T   9. F

CHAPTER 25 – Greece and Rome Collide
Test Book pages 85–87

True or False?
1. F   2. T   3. T   4. F   5. T   6. T   7. T   8. T   9. T   10. F

Multiple Choice
1. C   2. A   3. B   4. A   5. C   6. A   7. A   8. C   9. D   10. B

CHAPTER 26 – Marius and Sulla
Test Book pages 89–91

True or False?
1. T   2. T   3. T   4. F   5. F   6. T   7. T   8. T   9. F   10. F

Multiple Choice
1. B   2. C   3. A   4. A   5. C   6. A   7. D   8. B   9. D   10. C

CHAPTER 27 – The Rise and Fall of Julius Caesar
Test Book pages 93–94

True or False?
1. T   2. T   3. F   4. T   5. F   6. T   7. T   8. F   9. T   10. T

Matching
1. D   2. G   3. E   4. F   5. A   6. H   7. J   8. C   9. B   10. I

CHAPTER 28 – The Coming of Christ
Test Book pages 95–97

True or False?
1. T   2. T   3. T   4. T   5. F   6. F   7. F   8. T   9. T   10. F

Multiple Choice
1. C   2. A   3. C   4. D   5. B   6. B   7. C   8. D   9. A   10. B

CHAPTER 29 – Fishers of Men
Test Book pages 99–101

True or False?
1. T   2. F   3. F   4. T   5. F   6. T   7. T   8. F   9. T   10. F

Multiple Choice
1. C   2. A   3. B   4. B   5. D   6. B   7. D   8. A   9. C   10. C

CHAPTER 30 – Life Under the Julio-Claudians
Test Book pages 103–104

True or False?
1. F 2. T 3. F 4. T 5. T 6. F 7. T 8. T 9. F 10. T

Matching
1. G 2. B 3. F 4. A 5. E 6. H 7. D 8. J 9. I 10. C

CHAPTER 31 – Five "Good" Emperors
Test Book pages 105–106

Matching
1. G 2. B 3. F 4. A 5. C 6. E 7. H 8. D 9. J 10. I

True or False?
1. T 2. T 3. F 4. F 5. T 6. F 7. T 8. F 9. T 10. T

CHAPTER 32 – Collapse
Test Book pages 107–109

True or False?
1. T 2. T 3. F 4. T 5. F 6. T 7. T 8. F 9. T 10. F

Multiple Choice
1. C 2. D 3. A 4. B 5. C 6. B 7. A 8. B 9. D 10. C

CHAPTER 33 – The Growth of the Catholic Church
Test Book pages 111–113

True or False?
1. T 2. T 3. F 4. T 5. F 6. F 7. F 8. T 9. F 10. F

Multiple Choice
1. B 2. C 3. A 4. C 5. A 6. D 7. D 8. B 9. A 10. B

CHAPTER 34 – The Empire Divided
Test Book pages 115–116

True or False?
1. T 2. T 3. T 4. F 5. F 6. F 7. F 8. T 9. T 10. F

Matching
1. C 2. F 3. H 4. A 5. D 6. J 7. B 8. I 9. G 10. E

CHAPTER 35 – In This Sign, Conquer

Test Book pages 117–119

True or False?

1. T   2. F   3. T   4. T   5. T   6. T   7. T   8. F   9. T   10. F

Multiple Choice

1. A   2. B   3. D   4. A   5. D   6. B   7. C   8. D   9. A   10. C